A BUSINESS APPROACH TO CAULIFLOWER FARMING

Complete Entrepreneurial Step By Step Guide To Cauliflower Garden From Scratch

ZHURI HART

DISCLAIMER

This book is intended to provide general information and insights on adopting a business approach to farming. The content within is based on the author's knowledge and experiences up to the date of publication. It is essential to recognize that the field of agriculture is dynamic, influenced by various factors such as market conditions, climate, and regulatory changes.

Readers are advised to conduct thorough research, seek professional advice, and consider their unique circumstances before implementing any strategies or practices discussed in this book. The author and publisher disclaim any responsibility for the accuracy, completeness, or suitability of the information provided. The book is not a substitute for professional advice, and the author and publisher shall not be liable for any damages or losses arising from the use or reliance on the information presented herein.

Individual results may vary, and success in farming enterprises is contingent upon numerous variables. The author encourages readers to consult with relevant experts, agricultural extension services, and legal or financial professionals to tailor strategies to their specific needs and local conditions.

This book is not intended to be a comprehensive guide to all aspects of farming, and readers should exercise their judgment and discretion in applying the principles discussed. The author and publisher do not endorse any specific products, services, or companies mentioned in this book unless explicitly stated.

By reading this book, the reader acknowledges and accepts the inherent uncertainties in agricultural endeavors and agrees to use the information at their own risk.

TABLE OF CONTENTS

CHAPTER ONE 12

  FARMING CAULIFLOWERS INTRODUCTION 12

    CONTEXT AND SYNOPSIS...12

    THE VALUE OF GROWING CAULIFLOWERS 13

CHAPTER TWO 16

  KNOWING ABOUT CAULIFLOWER....................................16

    OVERVIEW OF BOTANY 16

    DIFFERENT TYPES OF CABBAGE..............................16

    CONDITIONS OF THE SOIL AND CLIMATE 17

    SEASONS OF GROWTH 18

CHAPTER THREE 20

  DEMAND ANALYSIS AND MARKET RESEARCH 20

    HOW TO SPOT MARKET TRENDS.............................20

    EXAMINING CUSTOMER CHOICES............................21

    EVALUATING REGIONAL AND WORLDWIDE DEMAND....21

    POSSIBLE DIFFICULTIES 22

CHAPTER FOUR 24

  ORGANIZING YOUR FARM FOR CAULIFLOWERS 24

    SELECTION AND SETUP OF THE SITE 24

    ROTATING CROPS AND PLANTING COMPANIONS 25

    FACILITIES AND GEAR..26

    BUDGETING AND FINANCIAL PLANNING 27

CHAPTER FIVE..28

  THE BEST WAYS TO GROW CAULIFLOWERS..................28

SELECTION AND GERMINATION OF SEEDS..........................28

PLANTING METHODS 29

MANAGEMENT OF WATER AND IRRIGATION 30

CONTROL OF PESTS AND DISEASES 30

CHAPTER SIX..32

CROP UPKEEP AND MANAGEMENT: 32

METHODS FOR WEED CONTROL 33

KEEPING AN EYE ON PLANT HEALTH 34

CHAPTER SEVEN 36

HARVESTING AND HANDLING AFTER HARVEST 36

ESTABLISHING THE IDEAL HARVEST TIME 36

TECHNIQUES FOR HARVESTING 37

CLASSIFYING AND EVALUATING 37

TRANSPORTATION AND STORAGE 38

CHAPTER EIGHT...40

MARKETING YOUR CAULIFLOWER COMPANY 40

BUILDING A STRONG BRAND IDENTITY AND USEFUL PACKAGING 40

FORMULATING A MARKETING PLAN...............................41

CREATING DISTRIBUTION ROUTES 42

DEVELOPING CONNECTIONS WITH CUSTOMERS...........42

CHAPTER NINE 44

ORGANIC AND SUSTAINABLE CAULIFLOWER FARMING 44

THE FOUNDATION OF SUSTAINABLE AGRICULTURE 44

CERTIFICATION FOR ORGANIC PRODUCTS.....................44

ENVIRONMENTALLY FRIENDLY METHODS 45

FULFILLING CUSTOMER REQUESTS FOR SUSTAINABILITY 46

ABOUT THE BOOK

The invaluable manual "A Business Approach to Cauliflower Farming" thoroughly examines the complexities of cauliflower production from a business standpoint. The book is designed to give readers a strong foundation in cauliflower growing, which makes it a valuable tool for both new and seasoned farmers.

To establish the scene, the introduction provides background information and an overview of cauliflower production, highlighting the crucial function this vegetable plays in the agricultural industry. The economic relevance of growing cauliflower and the rising demand for this adaptable vegetable is highlighted in the discussion of the importance of cauliflower farming. The book's goals are spelled out, assisting readers in developing a methodical comprehension of the material. Determining the target audience also guarantees that the content meets the unique requirements and preferences of farmers, business owners, and agriculture lovers.

In-depth information regarding cultivars, climatic and soil needs, and a botanical overview are all included in the second section, which explores the subtleties of cauliflower. By laying the foundations for later chapters, this foundational information guarantees a comprehensive comprehension of the cauliflower cultivation process.

Market research and demand analysis take the front stage, highlighting the practical approach used by the book. The market trends, consumer tastes, and local and global demand—all essential components of a profitable cauliflower-growing enterprise—that the readers learn about are insightful. Additionally, the section skillfully handles possible obstacles, giving farmers the insight they need to successfully negotiate a cutthroat market.

The reader is taken through each step of the planning, growing, managing, and marketing of cauliflower farming in the following parts. Every component, including budgeting, site selection, sustainable procedures, and post-harvest handling, is carefully considered. With an emphasis on efficiency and optimization, best practices, crop management strategies, and harvesting procedures are discussed.

The book's dedication to modern agricultural methods is reflected in the concluding section on organic and sustainable cauliflower cultivation. It looks at organic certification, eco-friendly practices, sustainable agriculture concepts, and meeting consumer desires for sustainability. The book is positioned as a useful resource in the changing field of responsible farming methods because of its forward-looking viewpoint.

Finally, "A Business Approach to Cauliflower Farming" is more than just a manual; it's a strategic toolkit that enables farmers to turn cauliflower farming into a sustainable and lucrative enterprise. This book acts as a catalyst for success in the rapidly expanding cauliflower sector by fusing theoretical insights with real-world applications.

CHAPTER ONE

FARMING CAULIFLOWERS
INTRODUCTION

CONTEXT AND SYNOPSIS

Brassica oleracea var. botrytis, or cauliflower, is a cruciferous vegetable that is both healthy and adaptable. Cauliflower is a Mediterranean vegetable that has become very popular all over the world because of its mild flavor and versatility in cooking. The plant is distinguished by a compact head of immature white flower buds encircled by verdant foliage. Cauliflower has grown to be a mainstay in many cuisines over time, improving both the culinary scene and the agricultural industry.

There is ample historical evidence that suggests cauliflower farming dates back to ancient times. Cauliflower was first grown in the Mediterranean and Asia, and as trade routes carried it to Europe and other regions, it finally became a mainstay in cuisines all over the world.

Over the ages, cauliflower has been cultivated and bred in different ways, giving rise to several distinct types with varying colors, sizes, and maturation times. The continuous practice of selective breeding and nurturing has been essential in creating the modern cauliflower.

THE VALUE OF GROWING CAULIFLOWERS

Cauliflower production has important economic, nutritional, and environmental implications in addition to its gastronomic value. Cauliflower farming boosts the agricultural economy and provides farmers with a means of subsistence. In areas where cauliflower is a prominent crop, the demand for the vegetable on both domestic and international markets has given farmers the chance to cultivate the crop commercially, which has boosted the local economy.

Cauliflower is a highly nutrient-dense vegetable that offers important vitamins, minerals, and dietary fiber.

Rich in folate, vitamins C and K, and other antioxidants, cauliflower is a nutritious supplement to a diet that is well-balanced. The growing trend of dietary preferences towards healthier options has resulted in an increased demand for nutrient-dense vegetables such as cauliflower, underscoring its significance in fulfilling the dietary requirements of various demographic groups.

Growing cauliflower is another way that sustainable agricultural methods are implemented. Cauliflower is a cruciferous vegetable that is resilient and flexible due to its capacity to grow in a variety of soil types and temperatures. In addition, compared to certain other vegetables, cauliflower is a crop that requires less pesticides and is generally low-maintenance. Its versatility and minimal input needs support sustainable farming methods, which are in line with the increased emphasis on ecologically friendly agriculture around the world.

The cultivation of cauliflower has a long history and is significant in many ways in the current agricultural environment. From its beginnings as a crop in ancient civilizations to its present status as a commercially successful crop, cauliflower has had a tremendous impact on the nutritional and economic well-being of people all over the world. Cauliflower farming continues to be an essential part of contemporary agriculture as the need for wholesome and environmentally friendly food sources grows.

CHAPTER TWO

KNOWING ABOUT CAULIFLOWER

OVERVIEW OF BOTANY

Scientifically speaking, cauliflower is called Brassica oleracea var. Brussels sprouts, cabbage, and broccoli are members of the Brassicaceae family, which also includes botrytis. This cruciferous vegetable is distinguished by dense heads or curds made up of compact, immature flower buds. The portion of the plant that can be eaten is the curd, which is made up of closely spaced florets. For millennia, people have been growing cauliflower and have selectively bred it to create numerous types with unique qualities.

DIFFERENT TYPES OF CABBAGE

There are many different types of cauliflower, and each has distinct characteristics related to size, color, and maturity. The most popular variety of cauliflower is traditional white, with a creamy-hued curd. Other variations include orange cauliflower, which is high in beta-carotene, and purple cauliflower, which gets its vivid violet color from the presence of anthocyanins. There are also green variations, including Romanesco cauliflower, which has a remarkable fractal-like look, and broccoflower, a combination of broccoli and cauliflower. These variants provide a range of culinary applications and health benefits.

CONDITIONS OF THE SOIL AND CLIMATE

A cool-season crop that does well in moderate weather is cauliflower. For best growth, it prefers daytime temperatures of 60 to 75 degrees Fahrenheit (15 to 24 degrees Celsius). Although it grows in a variety of soil conditions, well-drained, fertile soils with a pH between slightly acidic and neutral are best for cauliflower. Sufficient moisture is essential for growth, especially in the early phases when the plant is putting down roots. Mulching can contribute to a more ideal growing environment for cauliflower by controlling temperature and retaining soil moisture.

SEASONS OF GROWTH

The climate and the particular type being grown determine the length of the cauliflower growth season. Cauliflower is often planted as a spring and fall crop. It can also be grown in the winter in areas with moderate winters. Since cauliflower needs a certain temperature to produce its heads, timing is key. Poor curd growth can occur from planting too early in cold climates or too late in hot climates. Cauliflower production can only be effective if the growing season and local climate are taken into account when choosing cultivars. Furthermore, certain cultivars are developed to mature more quickly, giving growers more leeway in planting dates and expanding their possible harvest window.

CHAPTER THREE

DEMAND ANALYSIS AND MARKET RESEARCH

HOW TO SPOT MARKET TRENDS

A key component of market research is trend identification, which enables companies to stay ahead of the curve and adjust to the shifting tastes and behaviors of their customers. Market trends are influenced by several variables, such as evolving customer wants, advances in technology, modifications to laws and regulations, and new patterns in consumer behavior.

Monitoring these trends is an essential part of conducting comprehensive market research to comprehend industry dynamics and predict future changes. Businesses can acquire a competitive edge and strategically position themselves to meet changing client expectations by recognizing and utilizing market trends.

EXAMINING CUSTOMER CHOICES

Recognizing customer preferences is essential to developing goods or services that appeal to the intended market. Market researchers utilize several techniques, including focus groups, surveys, and data analytics, to investigate customer behavior and preferences. Examining elements such as product attributes, cost, brand loyalty, and general consumer experience is necessary to analyze these preferences. Businesses can improve customer happiness and loyalty by customizing their services to align with consumer expectations by collecting insights into what those customers value. This procedure helps in the formulation of successful marketing plans and the production of goods that satisfy the market's shifting needs.

EVALUATING REGIONAL AND WORLDWIDE DEMAND

For businesses to succeed in today's dynamic and linked marketplace, evaluating both local and global demand is crucial. Understanding the demands and preferences of the target market within a particular geographic area is the goal of local demand analysis. This can include local consumption trends that are influenced by economic, cultural, and demographic factors. However, evaluating worldwide demand necessitates a more comprehensive approach, taking into account elements like global market trends, trade regulations, and cultural diversity. Businesses can create complete strategies that incorporate regional differences and capitalize on broader market opportunities by examining demand on both scales.

POSSIBLE DIFFICULTIES

Researching the market also entails determining and addressing the obstacles that companies can encounter in the industry. These difficulties can be caused by several things, such as adjustments in customer attitudes, regulatory environment changes, economic downturns, and technology disruptions. Businesses can create backup plans and adjust their strategies to deal with uncertainty by thoroughly analyzing potential obstacles. It also makes it possible to take proactive steps that guarantee resilience in the face of unanticipated challenges. A crucial part of risk management comprehends potential obstacles, which enables companies to foresee and efficiently address the market's volatility. In addition to pointing out opportunities, effective market research gives companies the insight they need to anticipate and overcome potential challenges in their sector.

CHAPTER FOUR

ORGANIZING YOUR FARM FOR CAULIFLOWERS

SELECTION AND SETUP OF THE SITE

To ensure the best possible crop development and productivity, much consideration should be given to the selection and preparation of your farm before starting a cauliflower farm. Cauliflower grows best in well-draining, fertile soil that has a pH between slightly acidic and neutral. To start, test the soil to find out how much nutrients are there, then add the necessary amendments to produce the right growing conditions. To encourage strong plant development, pick a spot that receives full sun exposure. Adequate sunshine is another important consideration.

Furthermore, take into account the site's topography to guarantee appropriate water drainage and avoid waterlogging, which can negatively impact cauliflower roots. To make a neat and orderly planting location, proper site preparation includes removing rocks, weeds, and debris from the surrounding area. Throughout the cauliflower production cycle, the objective is to lay a foundation that facilitates simple access, good irrigation, and efficient pest management.

ROTATING CROPS AND PLANTING COMPANIONS

To keep soil healthy and stop pests and diseases from growing a successful crop rotation plan must be put into place. Given that cauliflower is a member of the brassica family, it is advisable to rotate crops to prevent soil-borne illnesses and nutrient depletion that may result from growing brassicas continuously in the same place. Cauliflower should be rotated with non-brassica crops to disrupt disease cycles and support a healthy soil environment.

Another important idea in cauliflower cultivation is companion planting. Cauliflower and companion plants that get along well can benefit from each other's natural pest control and enhanced nutrient intake.

For example, intercropping legumes with nitrogen-fixing plants like dill or chamomile can increase soil richness and help keep pests away from cauliflower plants.

FACILITIES AND GEAR

Purchasing the appropriate machinery and infrastructure is essential to your cauliflower farm's productivity and efficiency. High tunnels and greenhouses can increase the length of the growing season, shield crops from bad weather, and provide greater control over environmental factors. Make sure you have irrigation systems in place to deliver continuous moisture without waterlogging, whether through soaker hoses, drip irrigation, or other effective techniques.

Time and work can be saved during planting and cultivation by using mechanical tools like tractors, plows, and cultivators. Additionally, to protect young cauliflower plants from pests and inclement weather during their early stages of growth, think about investing in protective structures like row covers.

BUDGETING AND FINANCIAL PLANNING

Making a thorough financial plan and budget is crucial to your cauliflower farm's success. Start by calculating the initial costs, which should include equipment, seeds, infrastructure development, and land acquisition or leasing. Include continuing operating costs for labor, utilities, fertilizers, and insecticides. A well-planned budget facilitates effective resource allocation and the discovery of possible cost-saving opportunities.

To comprehend cauliflower demand and pricing patterns, have a look at market research. You can use this information to assess the scope of your business and establish reasonable revenue targets. Include a contingency fund in your budget to cover unforeseen expenses or changes in the marketplace.

CHAPTER FIVE

THE BEST WAYS TO GROW CAULIFLOWERS

SELECTION AND GERMINATION OF SEEDS

Making the right choice when it comes to cauliflower seeds is an essential first step in effective development. It is recommended that farmers select seeds from reliable vendors, making sure the seeds are disease-free and verified. Select hybrid kinds that are resistant to common illnesses and pests that affect cauliflower. Give top priority to seeds with a high rate of germination, as this will improve the crop's overall performance.

A healthy crop of cauliflower depends on proper germination. Begin by planting seeds in trays or a well-prepared seedbed that has been filled with a seed-starting mix that drains properly. Since cauliflower seeds are sensitive to changes in water availability, keep the moisture content constant during germination.

Enough light and warmth are also essential for encouraging consistent germination. To provide the best conditions for seedling development, think about employing a greenhouse or germination chamber.

PLANTING METHODS

Selecting the ideal planting time for your local climate is essential when transplanting cauliflower seedlings. Due to its preference for chilly weather, cauliflower is best planted in many areas in the early spring or late summer. Make sure the soil is pH neutral to slightly acidic, well-drained, and rich in organic matter.

Keep plants spaced appropriately to allow for sufficient air circulation, which helps ward against infections. Planting in rows makes it easier to harvest and perform maintenance duties. To reduce transplant shock, it is best to move seedlings during the cooler hours of the day. Furthermore, the nutrients required for early growth are supplied by sowing the soil with a balanced fertilizer.

MANAGEMENT OF WATER AND IRRIGATION

Throughout its growth cycle, cauliflower needs steady, balanced moisture. Sufficient irrigation is essential for stress reduction and ideal head development, particularly in arid times.

Since drip irrigation minimizes the risk of foliage diseases by delivering water straight to the root zone, it is frequently advised for the production of cauliflower.

Establish a regular watering routine; stay away from too much moisture, since this can cause fungal problems such as root rot. Mulching around plants aids in weed suppression and soil moisture retention. Keep a regular eye on the moisture content of the soil and modify your irrigation techniques according to the needs of the cauliflower crop and the weather.

CONTROL OF PESTS AND DISEASES

Managing pests and diseases well is essential to a successful cauliflower farming endeavor. It's crucial to regularly scout for pests like cabbage worms, caterpillars, and aphids. To manage pest populations, beneficial insects like ladybugs and predatory beetles can be incorporated as native predators.

Crop rotation techniques are one way to lower the danger of illnesses spread by the soil. Applications of fungicides might be required in areas where diseases like clubroot or downy mildew are common. To reduce the negative effects on the environment, use organic pest management techniques whenever feasible. Pests can be successfully repelled using neem oil, insecticidal soaps, and companion planting with plants like basil.

Growing cauliflower successfully requires careful seed selection, appropriate germination procedures, precise planting methods, effective irrigation, and attentive pest and disease management. Following these recommendations helps ensure a strong and healthy cauliflower crop, which in turn provides farmers with an abundant harvest.

CHAPTER SIX
CROP UPKEEP AND MANAGEMENT:
FERTILIZATION TECHNIQUES

An essential part of crop management is fertilization, which aims to maximize soil fertility and guarantee strong plant growth. Farmers use a variety of techniques to give crops the vital nutrients they need, increasing agricultural output and productivity. Utilizing chemical fertilizers, which are rich in potassium, phosphorus, and nitrogen—the three main elements essential to plant growth—is one popular strategy.

To enhance soil structure and promote microbial activity, organic fertilizers like compost and manure are also emphasized in sustainable agricultural methods. By using precision agricultural techniques, such as nutrient mapping and soil testing, farmers may customize fertilization practices to meet the demands of individual crops, avoiding misuse and reducing environmental effects.

Pruning and thinning: These two crucial crop management practices improve the general well-being and yield of plants respectively. Pruning is the deliberate removal of specific plant elements, including buds or branches, to promote desirable growth patterns, improve airflow, and stop the spread of disease.

In contrast, thinning entails removing extra stems or fruits to lower the plant's density. By ensuring that the remaining plant portions receive enough sunlight, nutrients, and water, both techniques aid in the optimization of resource allocation. In addition to increasing crop yield, appropriate pruning and thinning also helps with pest and disease control.

METHODS FOR WEED CONTROL

Since weeds can drastically lower yields and compete with crops for vital nutrients, controlling weeds is a critical part of crop management. Farmers use a variety of techniques to manage weeds, from chemical approaches like pesticide use to mechanical techniques like cultivation and plowing. Several tactics, including crop rotation, mulching, and cover crops, are combined in integrated weed management techniques to produce an all-encompassing and long-lasting weed control strategy. To reduce their dependency on synthetic herbicides and enhance the long-term health of their soil, organic farming systems frequently employ cultural techniques like hand weeding and the use of cover crops.

KEEPING AN EYE ON PLANT HEALTH

Vigilant monitoring of plant health is necessary for effective crop management to identify early indicators of illnesses, nutritional deficits, or pest infestations. Drones and other technological innovations allow farmers to efficiently examine enormous fields. Farmers may make well-informed judgments about applying nutrients and controlling pests with the use of routine visual inspections, soil testing, and plant tissue analysis.

Plant health can be monitored holistically with integrated pest management (IPM) tactics that combine chemical, cultural, and biological control techniques. To maximize agricultural output and quality, timely intervention based on precise monitoring guarantees that crops stay healthy throughout their growth cycle.

CHAPTER SEVEN

HARVESTING AND HANDLING AFTER HARVEST

ESTABLISHING THE IDEAL HARVEST TIME

One crucial component of agricultural operations that has a big impact on crop quality and output is figuring out when to harvest your crops. Growers need to find a balance between harvesting too soon, which can lead to undeveloped produce, and waiting too long, which can cause spoiling or overripening. When to harvest depends on several elements, such as the crop type, environmental circumstances, maturity indications, and planned usage.

To maximize nutritional content and flavor and guarantee that crops are chosen at their peak ripeness, maturity markers such as color, size, and texture are frequently examined. Furthermore, weather and temperature are major environmental elements that affect when the best time to harvest is.

TECHNIQUES FOR HARVESTING

Crops and farming systems differ in how they are harvested. Hand harvesting is a frequent method used for fruits and vegetables since it allows for thorough selection and less harm to the produce. In contrast, mechanical harvesting is more effective for large-scale operations—particularly when it comes to crops like legumes and grains. The choice of technique is contingent upon various circumstances, including crop qualities, production scale, and labor availability. Each approach has pros and cons. To increase productivity and decrease labor costs, modern technology like robotics and sensor-based systems are being incorporated into harvesting operations more and more.

CLASSIFYING AND EVALUATING

In the post-harvest handling process, sorting and grading are crucial stages that guarantee only premium food reaches consumers. Crops are sorted by being divided into different categories according to factors like size, color, and maturity. This stage ensures homogeneity in the finished product by removing parts that are undeveloped or faulty.

On the other hand, grading entails classifying the produce according to predetermined standards into several quality classes. This classification aids in the decision-making process for farmers, distributors, and consumers regarding the worth and planned application of the harvested commodities.

TRANSPORTATION AND STORAGE

The post-harvest handling process's essential elements of storage and transportation have a direct bearing on the crops' marketability and shelf life. The freshness and nutritional value of perishable goods are preserved with the aid of suitable storage facilities, such as cold storage or controlled environment storage. Controlling temperature, humidity, and ventilation are essential for keeping crops from spoiling and prolonging their shelf life. To guarantee that harvested produce arrives at its destination in the best possible shape, efficient transportation networks are necessary. A well-thought-out transportation strategy reduces losses and preserves the quality of the harvested products throughout transit, using everything from refrigerated trucks to cutting-edge packing techniques.

Successful agricultural operations depend on choosing the best time to harvest, using appropriate harvesting methods, putting in place efficient sorting and grading procedures, and making sure that products are stored and transported properly. In a market that is dynamic and competitive, these ideas work together to maximize crop quality, minimize losses, and satisfy consumer wants.

CHAPTER EIGHT

MARKETING YOUR CAULIFLOWER COMPANY

BUILDING A STRONG BRAND IDENTITY AND USEFUL PACKAGING

In the cutthroat world of cauliflower companies, these elements are essential to success. The brand encompasses the ideals and commitments that your small business stands for; it is more than just a name or logo. Developing a distinctive and enduring brand identity aids in setting your goods apart from those of rivals.

Make sure your target demographic connects with the messaging, visuals, and general tone of your brand. Additionally, spending money on eye-catching and useful packaging can improve shelf appeal and affect consumer perception. Strong and environmentally responsible packaging options could also fit well with the tastes of today's consumers, enhancing a brand's reputation.

FORMULATING A MARKETING PLAN

A carefully considered marketing plan is necessary for your cauliflower business to succeed. To begin with, gather information about your target market's preferences and the competitive environment by performing market research. Determine your USPs and utilize them to create persuasive marketing copy.

Email campaigns and social media are only two examples of the many marketing channels available on digital platforms. By making use of these resources, you can interact with potential clients and reach a larger audience.

Additionally, take into account conventional marketing strategies like participating in farmers' markets or forming alliances with nearby supermarkets. Maintaining a consistent message across several platforms is essential for strengthening your brand and increasing brand recognition.

CREATING DISTRIBUTION ROUTES

You must have effective routes of distribution if you want to make sure that your cauliflower goods are delivered to customers on time and under budget. Analyze various distribution strategies while taking the target market's features, cost implications, and geographic reach into account. To increase your reach, work with grocers, supermarkets, and specialized shops. Investigating internet marketplaces can also lead to new distribution channels, enabling clients to buy your cauliflower items from the convenience of their homes. Building trusting connections with retailers and distributors is essential to guaranteeing a seamless and dependable supply chain. Evaluate and improve your distribution networks regularly to adjust to shifting market conditions.

DEVELOPING CONNECTIONS WITH CUSTOMERS

Developing enduring relationships with clients is a continuous effort that calls for consideration and care. Establish channels for direct client communication, such as social media or a newsletter, to alert them of company developments, new items, and promotions. To promote brand loyalty and reward loyal customers, think about putting in place a loyalty program. Ask for and address consumer comments to show that you are dedicated to ongoing development. Establishing trust is crucial, and a good reputation may be enhanced by being open and honest about your sourcing methods, business principles, and your products. Personalized encounters, whether in-person or virtual, build a sense of community and brand loyalty among your customers.

CHAPTER NINE

ORGANIC AND SUSTAINABLE CAULIFLOWER FARMING

THE FOUNDATION OF SUSTAINABLE AGRICULTURE

The application of ideas based on ecologically conscious methods, promoting ecological balance, and guaranteeing the health of the crops and the surrounding ecosystem are the main focuses of sustainable and organic cauliflower farming. Long-term soil health is given priority, biodiversity is promoted, and environmental impact is kept to a minimum according to the principles of sustainable agriculture. By emphasizing the sustainability of resources and ecosystems, this strategy seeks to establish a positive link between agriculture and the environment.

CERTIFICATION FOR ORGANIC PRODUCTS

Obtaining organic certification is a crucial component in organic and sustainable cauliflower farming. To become certified as organic, one must follow the stringent rules and regulations established by regulatory organizations. Using organic inputs, avoiding synthetic fertilizers and pesticides, and implementing sustainable farming techniques are some examples of these requirements. By guaranteeing that no toxic chemicals are used in the cultivation of cauliflower, certification helps to promote environmental stewardship and healthier produce.

ENVIRONMENTALLY FRIENDLY METHODS

Sustainable cauliflower farming heavily relies on eco-friendly practices, which include a variety of methods designed to reduce the environmental impact of farming operations. Integrated pest management, crop rotation, and cover crops are often used tactics. Crop rotation breaks pest cycles and encourages nutritional balance in the soil, while cover crops assist reduce soil erosion, improve soil fertility, and control weeds. By combining biological and natural predators, integrated pest management lessens the need for chemical treatments.

FULFILLING CUSTOMER REQUESTS FOR SUSTAINABILITY

The adoption of organic and sustainable farming practices for cauliflower is primarily motivated by the need to satisfy customer aspirations for sustainability. The market for sustainably produced food has expanded recently, and consumers are looking for items that more closely reflect their values. In addition to helping to preserve the environment, farmers who meet this need also open up markets for cauliflower that is grown responsibly and ethically. A mutually beneficial relationship is fostered between farmers and customers via communication and transparency regarding sustainable practices.

The foundation of organic and sustainable cauliflower farming is a commitment to biodiversity, long-term sustainability, and environmental health. Cauliflower farming is approached holistically, going beyond simple crop growing, by pursuing organic certification, implementing eco-friendly practices, and being responsive to customer needs for sustainability. This paradigm shift toward sustainable techniques benefits the environment as well as conscious consumers who are looking for food options that are produced ethically and healthy.

.